PLASTIC LIFE

Giles L. Turnbull is a blind poet living in south Wales. His poems and articles have appeared in *Algebra of Owls*, *Poetry Wales*, and *Acumen*, amongst others, and in anthologies by Disability Arts Cymru, Three *Drops from a Cauldron*, and Nine Arches Press. He was shortlisted in the Live Canon International Poetry Competition in 2016 and the Bridport Prize in 2017. His debut pamphlet, *Dressing Up*, is published by Cinnamon Press.

ISBN: 978-1-917617-08-6

Cover designed by Aaron Kent

Cover image: © Krystsina / Adobe Stock

Edited and Typeset by Aaron Kent

Broken Sleep Books Ltd
PO BOX 102
Llandysul
SA44 9BG

CONTENTS

Plastic Life

Giles L. Turnbull

Broken Sleep Books

Cities can be lonely places, and in admitting this we see that loneliness doesn't necessarily require physical solitude, but rather an absence or paucity of connection, closeness, kinship: an inability, for one reason or another, to find as much intimacy as is desired.

— *The Lonely City* by Olivia Laing

CHAPTER I. SILENT NIGHTS

It was winter last we spoke
and everywhere I looked it seemed snowflakes were falling.
'Another year has ended,' you said,
'once again another year older.'
Everywhere I listened, hoping you were calling,
there was only snow and static;
all of this
falling after the mish-mash of footprints,
colder than the frosty pavements
and the quiet city sprawling.

'Another year has turned
and in this landscape sparse with friends it cannot get much colder.'
The trees with lights are only in other peoples windows,
carol singers at other peoples doors.

So on days like these I find myself by tracing backwards
from the plastic life of single servings and disposable wrappers,
to reach a point where you and I glanced upwards at the stars and said,
this is what happens all around us,
or rather that is what you said,
I lacked the words but nodded back
and knew that you had captured all that mattered;
I lacked the vision to see beyond what I could touch or taste
and did not memorise,
so I do not recall any of this
except in patchy moments
when I rub the dreams from the corners of my eyes,

before grabbing tea and toast
or, all too often, heading out the door
with nothing at all but the knowledge
that I need to be at work before the rest of London rises.

Under my desk I sometimes kick off my shoes
no one minds—
I share the end of the corridor only
with a catering pack of plastic cups
and forks and knives and something
someone told me once was used to clear the gutter.

Glancing round I sometimes think there are spies
who are armed with guns and gadgets
to separate the truth from the lies.
I expect them to be waiting as I walk through my door at night.
I sometimes think you'll have dinner ready—
a plate of steak and chips
or is that fries?
I forget what we should call them now.
I forget so much.

But I remember it was winter last we spoke.
I remember you telling me we were getting older.
Just before you followed the footsteps to another door,
which closed to keep you warmer.

I have my books
and many quiet nights on which to read them undisturbed,
except when people phone to sell me double glazing

or tell me my life should be insured.

Once there was heavy breathing

so I keep a whistle handy to break the bastards eardrums,

but hes never called again,

at least, not when I've been home.

CHAPTER II. TUMBLEWEED

I have always taken things as they come,
with a glimpse of hope,
sometimes pausing for a smoke
if they're not quite what I expect.
In smoking rooms I found captive friends -
I never see them now I've stopped.
I prefer night times away from folk,
after shutters have dropped,
leaving faceless shops,
while weary shoppers
cart their bargain basement offers
home, to show what they've bought
to whom they've got.

I sometimes walk,
you'll see me watching pigeons scrat for crumbs;
like them I shuffle off
leaving benches that remain empty once I've gone.
I tried to spend my evenings in,
even learning piano once
but on a plastic organ
with one-touch chords that promised to play along,
but even then I was all thumbs
and nothing resembling a tune.

So I walk and whistle, sometimes hum.
I never really wish to rush back home,
although the security is nice—
I always double lock the door.
In the living room an unshaded bulb
hangs above my beanbag throne.

CHAPTER III. WALKING ON THE GROUND

I am not well
but never medically ill.

I found medicine for loneliness
but not in pills.

Have you seen those backscratchers
shaped like hands?

I need one of those
to scratch this itch

which I cannot reach,
because I was never taught posh speech,

though my best teachers let me dream
and helped me understand what life means.

I think that helps me
now I'm walking on the ground

with my own feet;
I just wish sometimes

I could try somebody else's shoes
and have the luxury of time

to reflect on what I choose
when answering the questions that I meet

head-on;
when lost and found

lock horns
with win or lose.

CHAPTER IV. TUNNEL VISION

This is The Tube—
underground rail
sardine tins on wheels
with brakes that squeal
like the fresh-faced dawn
being greeted by a cockatiel,
where everyone is third class
and the armpit smell of suited men
invades your nose;
we are fellow commuters—
we travel together but never meet.

But I travel early to miss as much of those
inhumane conditions
as is humanly possible.
Sometimes I fail and then I wonder
why I live this life—
I honestly do not know.
I'd miss the blackness
punctured by roundels that signify
other destinations exist
for other people
with other lives.

Even when the route is quiet
and passengers aren't squashed against the doors,
I'd give it all up in an instant
if I took the time to wonder

why I think I love this life I sought.
Was it just some blunder
That placed me here?
I have my suspicions—
I remember the day
I caught an otherwise empty tram
from Wimbledon to God-knows-where
and you got on
and we sat in adjacent seats—
once again, as I always have
I thought we were a most unlikely pair.

But that was then.
This is Victoria,
a statement of fact.
Familiar in the morning.
Waiting in the evening.
This is seven o'clock
and the Bank-bound businessmen
are Watching the pretty girls get off at Oxford Circus,
because that is what they do
time and time again.

But Victoria is always here.
This is Victoria.
This is The Tube,
daily medicine for loneliness
as thousands of people use
every morning.

CHAPTER V. ALPHABET SOUP

I work with three people,
let's call them
X (Ex), Y (Why), and Z (Zed)
We share identical desks,
are career-focused,
ambition-led

and we all feel we're missing
too many hours in bed,
but we give that up

because it pays the rent. .
It's survival of the quickest
though we all dream of something new.

Lunch is a sandwich or a bag of crisps;
Z (zed) just sips
bottled water and sighs,

like there's nothing in this world
to tempt her,
nothing to persuade her to try

a crisp or bread with a hint of butter.
Nothing on earth
could make her feel worse

about her weight—
she used to be size eight
and I assure her she still looks wonderful

and has the most magical eyes—
deep as whirlpools
and brown like oak,

but too often I joke
and she never believes anything I say...
she thinks I play the fool too often.

In London we sell advertising space
because slogans can be put

and can be seen
in every conceivable place

by a million pairs of eyes
that rarely shut.

Days are such a pace
that commuter life will always buy,

if it sees a pretty face
eulogise, 'You need to try

these amazing things
to make your life complete, as did I.'

They're the same people who believe
energy drinks will help you fly.

Just like fools,
busy people and hard-earned money

are easily parted,
and the phone for advertising

never lets up—
there's always someone pitching

the light-speed sneaker,
the bottomless cup.

This is my universe
or at least the world in which I live.

This is flashpoint city,
tip of the ice cube,

and I know it has consumed
everything I have to give.

CHAPTER VI. TWO SIDES TO A STORY

Memories of you, now and then,
swirl amongst the latte mornings,
cappuccino lunchtimes,
espresso evenings,
but always in takeout
always carry-away in plastic.
Prêt-à-porter.

I do not think anything is permanent,
an off-the-peg replacement always fits.
and that is how I'm glued together,
out of myriad disposable bits.
One moment I hold something fragile in my hand
the next...

And, just like that, I felt
like from my life you removed yourself
not once, not twice,
but every time of asking;
every time I panicked you stepped outside.

I've never been convinced it wasn't all a lie,
just like the tears you made me think you'd cried
by leaving crumpled tissues in the bin;
with hindsight I wonder why we ever even tried.

In your words:

We talk too little
you and I.
We talk of the weather,
groceries and, 'whats up?'
and that, for you,
seems to be excitement enough.
'Goodnight,'
we sometimes say
but never kiss
There's too much wrong to stay.

In mine :
This is anger
or maybe depression.
This is getting it
out of my system.
This is shouting
louder than I need to hear.
This is the doubt of everything
I loved and thought was near
from day one
and still counting.
This is the end of an era,
short as it was
it is over.

...Or,

as I actually said,

'Goodbye.'

(I lack the words.)

My speech was a monologue to the door

that you had used and left forsaken.

No one knew that I had spoken

a poetic farewell,

and no one will.

At that moment I was broken.

CHAPTER VII. AIN'T MISBEHAVIN'

I have nasty habits
I bite my nails
chew gum
forget details
avoid the sun.
I had friends
who went off the rails
whilst still quite young—
never meant to be bad
they were just seeking fun
and I got left behind
whilst many of them wound up in jail.
I just have bad habits.

CHAPTER VIII. SOFT SALE, HARD SELL

And so I digest my lunch
without exactly knowing how.
Everything hides
behind the mechanics,
the marketing,
the glossy lies.
We simply have a hunch
and serve it up with metaphorical fries
and a little bit of WOW.

I am not keeping count
of friendships that cannot mend.
I keep my insecurities close at heart,
striking out calendar squares
when paranoia starts the day
and, only if I sleep,
finds end;
I am the sum of frighteningly small parts
playing a game with rules that will not bend.

My colleagues and I,
find images to connect
with how you feel, infect
your brain with a tune to hum.
We give a soft edge to the steel,
plant a seed within your ear.
Even if we only piss you off
that annoyance may be the crazy deal.
The battle waiting to be won.

Ding, ding

I have no idea
what root gave growth to fear,
what fed the shoot and nurtured
the growing plant,
and whether insanity was the fruit.
For all I know this body may be
only a vessel for the juice.
Side-lined between love and distraction,
somewhere I am torn and bruised.

We will tell you exactly what you need to hear
and help you recognise
the affordability of the price.
We connect product with prayer
blur the distinction between victim and vice.
We are the thermometer for reaction,
the barometer for advice.
In salesman hell
nobody plays fair.

I cannot now separate
painting from Polaroid,
vision from view.
Could I see the truth
if I stopped and thought it through?
I do not belong
I sing but the words are wrong,
I put them to tunes from other songs
and find askew harmonics.

When you think you think you understand
think again.
Find the time to ask
what was code,
where were the clues
and who owns the plan.
It's a frosty path
with precarious twists,
fighting explosive demand.

CHAPTER IX. ON THE TURNING OF THE CUP

I still look for you
between every blade of grass
between the flagstone cracks
of unsympathetic streets

and there you are
oblivious to my stare

So I walk on
And eat beans on toast
or egg on toast
with a pot of tea

At single tables
In the cheapest places.

I upend my cup
Turn it counter-clockwise
and look for the future
on the bone china base

as I learned from my nan
in halcyon days.

Your face congeals at the top
while on the side
a butterfly flutters its wings.
In the depths, two solitary birds fly.

The remnants of my life
spelled out in loose-leaf tea

I am your jetsam,
invisible
as you pass the windows of the cheapest places.
in whose windows you would not deign to look.

CHAPTER X. REPENTANCE

Perhaps you knew—
I'm sure you did,
you never could resist;
like when I returned to find you supping ice-chilled Bolly,
looking like butter wouldn't melt.
In your laugh I heard
a touch of the demonic
bitch.

That's how I saw it
because until then I'd felt
you had no fault.
But you'd guessed that I was lonely
or had had enough
of living
according to the cards that I'd been dealt.

You were right. I had. I'm sorry.
I'm sorry for both of us.
For both of us
you finding me was bad
though you never seemed to stop to let that worry—
femme fatale of dreams.
My life was an open book
and with just one look you knew what you would find
amongst the muck.

However unconvinced I look

I do not want you back.

Too much has passed.

You ran for the mountains

I sinned with the city.

I know, I lack a certain strength of character.

You were right not to come back

although perhaps...

no, the deck was always stacked.

CHAPTER XI. TASTE

The afternoon solidifies
from a sea of paper, digitised
on flat screen, database-categorised:
A-list... B-list... other.
The rich and famous,
the minor celebs,
and the faces from Big Brother,
cast enticingly on todays front page and tomorrows poster;
very few favourably age
and fewer still survive.

But the queue for billboards ends in slogans
and pictures that scream a thousand words
with faces in all the high-vis places—
as much about being seen as being heard.
Whether serenely subtle or brazenly bold,
it's always an addictive poison
and no one is giving away the cure.
I, like you, was once a victim
and the taste still lingers as I walk away.
I am not a spiritual soul.

CHAPTER XII. SPEAKING TO THE BIRDS

My train is as late as I am old,
if minutes were years.
I am being eaten from within
by an insatiable black hole,
consuming everything except my fears,
leaving me on platform edges
thin and cold—
one day my train will come.

One day my train will come
I hear the rusty Tannoy apologise
to commuter ears
but this is no surprise—
amongst us there are some
reassured seeing pigeons we recognise
(this one I call Francis, that one Clare)
I always meet their eyes.
To all else I am numb.

To all else I am numb

And as sure as ink on paper,
blood on empty battlefields
after the fighting has died,
these tears would not dry
if any of us had but the strength to cry.
How do you who do not know this
see us through your eyes?
What have we become?

What have we become?

When I search for religion I find it here,
high above the rails.
A truth, no matter what you believe—
the trains arrive and then they leave,
and in the canopy
the pigeons,
like prophets, speaking in foreign tongues.
praise be.

Praise be

CHAPTER XIII. CAPRICORN

Oh, this is Capricorn,
I know you didn't see her creeping up,
she excels at that—
materialising when least expected,
weaving tripwire-like to halt you in your tracks,
manicuring her nails on the papered walls,
the bed, the carpets, a trousered leg, the chairs
all are victims to her claws;
Her tail
swishes a story in semaphore.

Before I leave the house or head to bed
I pause
to put down food for my favourite cat,
'who's my faaaaaaaay-vourite cat?' as she likes to be called.

This is my front door, hewn
from mahogany or solid oak...
or it could have been
if I lived beyond the border where grey meets green,
in places maybe where you watch the boats
on the banks beside the Thames
and, on quiet nights, enjoy the moon.
Where you know the people as more than folk,
possibly as friends.

Where you do not feel the city permeate every pore,
a place beyond the intestinal Tube line ends.

Where you may even find time to smile
and space to mend.

My door is a truism:
Unidentifiable, Plastic,
Vague and Colourless,
the checkpoint standing between inner soul and city rock.
With every venture taken outside,
I find I'm coping slightly worse
beyond the bulletproof UPVC, double-locked.

Hence I'm always thrilled to see Capricorn come evening
anticipating the little knock by which she knows I'm home.
With her the house is never empty
and I am not alone.
Her welcome back greeting, with yawn and yowl,
a transient scowl relaying, 'Where've you been?'
Sometimes I think that no one understands except for her;
I wonder what others would hear
if they simply paused and, to their ear, they cupped a hand.

Capricorn,
inspecting everything
owning the old, adopting the new.
I love her poise, her elegance,
her voice persuasive.
whether stating her point of view or telling me what she needs.
she senses when I'm sad
and purrs to let me know shes pleased that I am there.

Capricorn spends many person-hours
in sun, rain, wind all and any weather,
dallying amongst the pots of kitchen herbs I raise together,
she seems to like the way they smell,
the way they dance.
Outside, she finds shade and shelter
and sees details I often miss
because I cast only an uneducated glance—
I did not, for example, realise
that every day, flowers kiss
even though I believe
in fairy-tale romance.

I adore the daffodil-drenched spring,
flushed with all the promise that begins
as buds break soil,
burstingly flamboyant,
unrepentant against the relentless swings
that encapsulate the simplest things,
the questions from which too many people hide,
because the old stories survive.

This is my means of getting through
the doors and the days,
of slowing down the seconds
and lengthening the breaks,
of finding space to grow
in a world relentlessly pressing in.

CHAPTER XIV. GRAVITY

What colour are my insides?
I do not like to think,
with the cigarettes I used to smoke and all the tea I drink
I don't suppose I'll ever know.

What colour are my eyes when I laugh and joke?
Are they dark on days when my heartbeat quickens,
my chest tightens
and I begin to sink?

Are they blue to match the skies
when I recognise the fragrances I knew
before, slipping through
yet manage not to choke?

Looking out from London's Eye,
no greater leveller for a covert spy,
peering beyond landmark bridges
at rivers of traffic and dams of buildings.

Up here,
divorced from sound and situation,
I am close enough to touch the clouds
with fingertips and fascination.

From such great height the sequences of fairy steps
are vanishingly small,
teasing patterns
from the to and fro.

With tranquil pulse and tidal habit
the days and nights metronomically
stamp every decision,
the separations and the collisions.

This is the machinery of government.
It's simply what happens all around us,
it need not expand to explanation
and rarely do I find it does.

The mechanics of a universe keeping its secrets close,
going about its chores,
like a child kicking a ball,
obeying the same laws—

the decisions are made behind closed doors.
Just like me,
the apple had no choice
but to fall.

CHAPTER XV. MOVING ON

Today began
the way that you and I had ended
that day we signed and went our ways:

I offered him my hand.
I guess there's always a kind of death in the dissolving
whether sudden or planned.

The way that we that's you and I,
politely smiled and promised to write
after the crossing of ts and the dotting of is.

On this day
where nobody really knows what to say
nor where to stand.

He was dressed like me:
black suit, black tie, black shoes
same damned haircut.

He wouldn't meet my eyes,
the moment raw,
the wedding ring, which I still wore,

I guess it caught a nerve
the way bad news will always surprise
first time heard.

We overcame the awkwardness
of shaking an unfamiliar hand;
I assumed you'd have said

in lighter moments,
'Oh, my ex used his left,'
I guess there wasn't time.

Her family kept a distance—
no change there,
no unfamiliar pretence,

if it hadn't been the pen
they'd have stabbed me with the sword;
they abhorred

my lack of words,
which suited me fine—
I preferred to be ignored.

Stutteringly the minutes led towards
him and me.
Your mother blamed us both
She understood us less
than we did your disease.

Me and him
standing like sentinels.
He and I, infused
in the intoxicating liquor

of a day, brewed
like off-kilter coffee,
strong and black and bitter.

And that's pretty much the way it ends,
your mother taking the stand:
'it was your fault. You were the damage.'

I told her straight,
'Your daughter loved me,
finished my sentences,
manicured my nails,'
and then, I couldn't resist,
'We used to fuck like rabbits.'

You'd been gone two seconds
already I could feel you turning in your grave.
I didn't really expect anybody would understand.

You and I always knew,
failing to bite my tongue
was another of those bad habits.

CHAPTER XVI. VERTIGO

The flowers that mean that life goes on
lie hewn and un-watered,
pushed to one side,
shouting that time and tide
never really wait
for us to walk,
catch up,
and fall again.

The preoccupations of people passing,
gazes casting
shadows like a cloak across my name,
mistook silence for an answer
when no one even breathed
much less spoke
or sought to blame.

The outstretched optimism
of those who still expect a hand to grasp their hand,
but who would know where it began
let alone where it might lead
or end?

Challenging the curse
that seeks to damn,
on a kerbside clifftop, hesitating,
I tottered
and felt a push

to join the non-stop traffic
that shouts that life goes on
because it must.

LAY OUT YOUR UNREST

.

www.ingramcontent.com/pod-product-compliance
Lightning Source LLC
LaVergne TN
LVHW092323080426
835508LV00040B/1269